'Waiting for the Hoppers' Train', 22 October 1892.

THE
Archive Photographs
SERIES

THE ANNUAL HOP
LONDON TO KENT

Compiled by
Hilary Heffernan

CHALFORD

First published 1996
Copyright © Hilary Heffernan, 1996

The Chalford Publishing Company
St Mary's Mill, Chalford,
Stroud, Gloucestershire, GL6 8NX

ISBN 0 7524 0379 6

Typesetting and origination by
The Chalford Publishing Company
Printed in Great Britain by
Redwood Books, Trowbridge

Hopping down in Kent.

Contents

*This book
is dedicated to my children
Madeleine and John Heffernan,
who have long been my inspiration and motivation*

305·9633

My gratitude is expressed to Gloria Morris for her support and help in acquiring the pictures and collections from east Kent and to my son John, who patiently checked the proofs.

My appreciation goes to Sidney Fagan, Joyce Bullimore, Pam Price and Mr and Mrs Adam Champneys, Lamberhurst, for their advice and support, and to the many ex-Hopping contributors without whose pictures this book would not have been produced

Introduction

'Me and my family have great memories of the hop-picking days. I am eighty years old now, but the old days are so vivid. I was 4 yrs old and used to go hopping. When I was eleven I was old enough to share a bin with an adult. We used to get up early… by candlelight. 6 o'clock mornings to set off to walk …2 or 3 miles… and work until 5, then walk back home, very tired. We took with us piles of bread and dripping and jam as the smell of hops made one hungry. Our poor fingers were black and stunted by the hops. We were told if we were good children and worked hard we could have our brown boots for Sunday wear. Black, button up with a button hook for week-day. So I can tell you we were grateful for hop-picking.' So wrote Mrs Phyllis Ash, one of the many contributors to this book, which attempts to link London, the villages across north Kent associated with hops and the many hundreds of families who traditionally took on picking every autumn. It became a way of life: a bright spot of the year; a way of earning enough money for winter boots or a decent Christmas dinner. Names are deliberately named; they are a small part of British history. This book intends, not only to show where pickers came from, their circumstances and why they were keen to travel far into the Kent countryside to find brief seasonal work on the hop farms, but also something of the history and business of hop-picking and as an instrument to help ex-hopping families who lost touch to contact each other once more and keep alive the memories. Although here we deal only with north and mid Kent, this was not the only hop-picking area. Other localities in other counties used roughly the same system for garnering the crop fundamental to good British beer-making.

Seeking original pictures, I appealed through London and Kent newspapers for pre-1950 hop-picking photographs, expecting to hear mainly from Eastenders, and was delighted to receive letters from a far wider field: London, Kent, Devon, Canada; Ex-hoppers, each wanting to share their anecdotes and firmly pointing out that London's Eastend supplied only a small part of the story. Some hoppers came from nearby Kent villages: many retired to live in these same villages at the end of their working lives.

In August, 1995 I was invited to a hop-pickers' reunion in Horsmonden; a delightful trip of nostalgia where ex-hoppers talked over the old times. Some memorable names were Pam Price and family from Deptford, Joe Lucy, Pat Greenwood, Harry and Ethel Langford now in their 70s, Linda and Vicky Granger, Peggy Ball, the Goodwins, Fowlers; all well-known Deptford families. As our coach rolled down through the Kent countryside all the old songs were sung. This traditional song, words courtesy of Pam Price, was the most popular:

'If you go down hopping,
Hopping down in Kent,
You'll see old Mother Riley
A-putting up her tent.
   With an ee-aye-o, ee-aye-o,
ee-aye-ee-aye-o.

They say that hopping's lousy,
I don't believe it's true,
   We only go down hoppin'
To earn a bob or too,
   With an……..etc.'

There were many verses and several versions, some cheekier than others. Lilian Heath supplied words to the following:

'We are the Deptford (Peckham, Bermondsey etc) girls,
We are some of the lads.
We know our manners,
Spend all our tanners.

We are respected wherever we go.
We go marching down the Old Kent Road,
Doors and windows open wide.
If you see a copper come
Hit him in the eye and run,
We are the Deptford girls.'

The hop is a perennial plant, either male or female. More female plants are grown as only female flowers of hops are used for brewing. According to some sources, hops are a member of the nettle family, while Pears *Cyclopedia* (1950) claim it is a member of the mulberry family. The bitter flavour comes from the hop-flowers' resin and tannin which is also a preservative. Although hops (*humulus lupulus*) were used for beer from ancient times on the Continent, they were generally regarded as unwholesome in Britain. Henry VIII, though fond of ale, refused to quaff any drink made from hops. In fact hops were not cultivated commercially in England until around the middle of the sixteenth century.

Early historical and literary references are fairly abundant. Pliny the Elder (AD 1) described hops and their cultivation in his *Historia Naturalis* published AD 77, based on his scientific survey of the area around Germany and Austria. Hops were trained up poles from early times; during the sixteenth century Thomas Tusser, landowner at Cattawade, Suffolk, wrote several instructive books on farming, including *Five Hundred Pointes of Good Husbandrie* (1557) which covered the care of hops. He wrote 'Get into thy hopyard, for now it is time/To teach Robin Hop on his pole how to climb.' (xii.17). If you are looking for a sound reason to partake of the amber brew you cannot do better than refer to the seventeenth century herbalist, Nicholas Culpeper, who wrote 'The hop runs to a great height, climbing up and twisting round the poles which are placed for its support; the branches are rough and hairy... (with) vine like leaves... on tops of the stalks grow clusters of large, loose, scaly heads of a pale greenish yellow colour when ripe, and smell pretty strong... It is under the dominion of Mars. This will open obstructions of the liver and spleen, cleanse the blood, loosen the belly, cleanse the reins from gravel, and provoke urine. The decoction of the tops cleanses the blood, cures the venereal disease, and all kinds of scabs, itch and other breakings out of the body; as also tetters, ringworms, spreading sores, the morphew, and all discolourings of the skin... kills worms, brings down women's courses, and expels urine...yellow jaundice, headache... agues that arise from choler and blood. The young hop sprouts (...March or April...) being mild, if boiled and served up like asparagus, are a very wholesome as well as pleasant tasted spring food. They purify the blood and keep the body gently open.' Christopher Smart, an eighteenth-century poet of Shipbourne, nr. Tonbridge, sometime suspected of being insane due to his uncontrollable habit of loudly spouting the Scriptures, wrote *The Hop-Garden*, two books in blank verse about life and work in the hop-fields. Charles Dickens was familiar with Kentish hopfields and would have seen them on his travels about the county. He mentions them in both *Pickwick Papers* and *David Copperfield*, while George Orwell, in *The Clergyman's Daughter*, mentions the Hop-pickers inability to strike for more pay. '...Strikes were practically impossible... the farmers had the pickers in a cleft stick; but ... the low price of hops was the root of the trouble... few of the pickers had more than a dim idea of the amount they earned. The system of piecework disguised the low payments... two pence a bushel.'(Ch.II.p109). More recently is H.E. Bates' popular *Darling Buds of May* starring David Jason, 1994, on television, set among the hopfields of Kent.

The poor from early times commuted to seasonal hop work in the fresh Kent countryside air, glad to escape over-crowded London's slums and smoke for a few weeks before winter set in. Men took their families down one late August weekend, travelling by train, horse and trap, bike, rag-and-bone cart, coal cart or on foot, pushing wooden, home-made handcarts containing all the family would need for their stay-bedding, pots and pans, food, even chairs and a tin bath. Leaving the women and children to settle in they travelled back home ready to continue their usual work early Monday morning. Each weekend they left for the hop gardens

8

to join their families, Families saved for months beforehand, scrimping each week's rations to set aside a little flour, tea, dried food ready to take down with them. Often several families from one street occupied one row of huts. Meals were cooked outside on open fires; children, washed in tin baths or under a hose in the open air. Single people were invited to eat with families; no-one was left on their own. Most families returned year after year to the same farm, occupying the same huts.

Despite tough, tiring work, long hours in the fields and stained, sore hands this was the family's annual paid holiday and they made the most of it with evening sing-songs and home-spun entertainment, often held at the nearby village pub. Some of these still retain the old names: 'The Malt Shovel', the 'Gun and Spitroast', 'The Hop Pole', 'The Hop Bine'…

Trains were provided for Hoppers, who crowded into London Bridge station to catch the early morning Special to Paddock Wood, or nearest station to their hop farm. The platform seethed with families, excited children, cardboard suitcases, tea-chest or converted pram handcarts and roughly wrapped bundles of last-minute, nearly-forgotten belongings. Most farmers allowed women and children to travel down a week before picking began to prepare their huts. Accommodation varied considerably; one ex-hopper recalls the farmer clearing out his pigs from the huts only days before the workers arrived. Families set to with scrubbing brushes, enamel buckets of water, lysol soap and even whitewash before moving in. Soon net curtains appeared at gaping windows, privacy blankets hung in open doorways; handcarts were converted to tables, wooden boxes to cupboards while old grandma or grandpa sat in the only chair. Candles or hurricane lamps provided light and a Valor paraffin stove kept the hut warm on chilly nights. The privvy was either an open latrine or a wood hut with wooden seat over an open hole or bucket which had to be emptied daily. Some hoppers' huts were purpose-built of stone, wood or corrugated iron. These were usually fitted with a large double bunk for mum and dad, a lower bunk for the children, and a space at the foot of the top bunk for baby.

Freedom of the countryside was paradise to children used to dirty city streets. While it was important they worked hard with the hop-picking (those bushel baskets took a lot of filling) there was still time aplenty for exploring open fields and woods. Most farmers were generous with surplus apples, tipping them in a heap on the common for families to help themselves. Apple scrumping was great fun, but with some farmers it could be dangerous if caught: the culprit and family risked being dismissed, having to find their own way back to London, losing their place at the hop garden and possibly all money earned that season.

The bines grew four to a set, or root. Women and children pulled down the bines (although on some farms such as Whitbread's, this was the binmen's job) stripping the hops into pole and canvas bins. The measurer then measured how many bushel basketsful of hops were in each bin and these were credited to the pickers by means of tokens, tally records or record books, according to the farm. Pole pullers, usually men, were responsible for hooking down the crowns (topmost part of the bines) if they broke off and were caught on the string: nothing was wasted. They were responsible for the pickers in their own group, moved the bins when a row was done, filled and carried the pokes and ensured the area was left tidy. Poke fillers (with hops from the bins), carters driving horse-drawn carts loaded with tightly-packed pokes to oast houses where they were spread on the roasting floor, tallymen, dryers etc were all jobs usually done by regular farm workers who looked after the hop garden all the year round. Overhead wires and strings were tied in place in the winter by men balancing head high on wooden stilts. Hop-classers used a special tool; a purpose-sharpened knife used to cut samples from selected bags. This was an expert's job; sustained high quality was important when selling to the brewery. Sometimes, sulphur was added to the drying wood fires to give hops the desired flavour and colour. When the kilns were lit, roasting hops could be smelled all over the farm. The work was hard, but those who went and took part never forgot their experiences and recall them as the happiest days of their childhood.

The original hops were Fuggles, larger and more full bodied than today's varieties. Kent's hop gardens mainly covered three areas in North and mid Kent, although farms were located further south around Tonbridge, Lamberhurst and into Sussex. Three major locations centred on

Paddock Wood, Maidstone and Canterbury forming a corridor across North Kent. Once mechanised hop-picking came into force, in the mid 1950s, there was no longer any need for farmers to employ large workforces. A few non-mechanized farms lingered into the 1960s but for the most part, 'hopping' and its hoppers faded into history and many once-lively small villages faded with them. While some oast houses have been converted to private homes a few remain in their original state, conforming to our romantic picture of Kent rural life as depicted in the late Rowland Hilder's evocative paintings.

Pay varied across the farms, though only by a 1d per bushel. Sometimes it was better to stick with a farmer paying slightly less, where living quarters were comfortable and the family friendly, than to go to a higher-paying farmer who didn't cater so well for his pickers. The money usually went to pay for the children's new winter boots, or to save for something special for the family.

There was the occasional serious accident, but pickers mainly suffered from sore fingers, dermatitis, fingers blackened by the hops, or cuts sustained stripping hops from the bines. Where there were several hop farms surrounding a village employing large numbers of seasonal hoppers, a village Hopper's Hospital was set up, run by the Salvation Army, W.V.S., British Red Cross, local doctor or Capuchin friars from St. Fidelis church in Erith.

Although Chapter One depicts mainly South and East London, these scenes are representative of manufacturing and labouring families' housing in London as a whole in the late nineteenth and first half of the twentieth centuries. Hoppers came from all over London and environs.

Hopping has passed into history, yet it was a way of life still within easy living memory: Many forty and fifty year olds happily recall hop-picking as the most memorable time of their childhood. Their vivid recollections of the warmth and camaraderie are engendered by working in close harmony with friends, of freedom and the healthy life offered by working in hop gardens far from the smells, noise and dirt of a big city.

If you want to see working hopgardens as they were it is well worth visiting the Kent Museum of Rural Life at Lock Lane, Sandling, Cobtree near Maidstone where hops are still picked in the traditional way (in September). The Museum has a unique collection of hopping memorabilia. You can still see how pickers lived by visiting their huts, a traditional hop field, working oast house, tools and regular exhibitions. Nearby, Whitbread's Hop Farm still houses the beautiful shire horses used to haul brewers' carts, now mainly used to exhibit at country shows or in parades. Both museums have fine displays of hop-picking life, including implements, farming tools and machines.

Purbrook Street, South London. 1939. Like today's inner-city children, there was nowhere for town and city children to play except in the streets. Although cars were few, there were dangers from abandoned, unsafe houses, bomb sites, horse-drawn carts, trams and lorries.

As everyone knew everyone else living in their street and most of their business, discipline tended to be strict for children. It was normal for neighbours and passing policemen to reprimand any child caught misbehaving and report them to their parents, which tended to keep waywardness in check.

One

Why Make the Long Journey to Kent for Poor Pay?

With many families living on the bread-line, poor housing, low pay, long hours often in noisy, hazardous working conditions, large families to feed, clothe, shoe and provide for, concern about paying the rent collector or staving off the bailiffs. With worries like these it was bliss to escape into the quiet countryside for a few weeks to forget their troubles, especially when hop pickers could earn a few extra 'bob' to ease the family budget. Every September, London station was filled to overflowing with families and their belongings packed in home-made, rickety handcarts ready for their annual hopping holiday. Despite being expected to commence work at 6am and work through to 6pm with only three short breaks the hoppers looked forward to their 4-6 weeks in the hop gardens of Kent as the highlight of their year.

Housing for London's poor was in 'back-to-back' terraced houses, or tenement blocks such as Queen's Buildings, Scovell Road, south London. Often kept in poor repair, some dwellings were flea-ridden slums. Periodically, in attempts to sanitise the tenements, board officials ordered flea and bug-infested mattresses be thrown into the courtyards and burned. Children of families living in such places were prone to TB, rickets and fevers. Few families could afford medical help, although some doctors, such as medical pioneering humanitarian Dr Alfred Salter, alleviated the problems by setting up free medical centres and solariums.

Grannie Easom, a regular hopper, enjoying sitting out in the sun on the stairs of her tenement flat with her grandchildren, George Shrieve and his cousin Kate.

After London was bombed in World War Two, wiping out many of the tenement blocks, the Shrieve family counted themselves lucky to be given a 'Prefab' (prefabricated house). These were intended to last ten years, but some are still in use fifty years on. A prefab, furnished as it would have been during and after the war, can be seen at Duxford Airfield, Cambs.

One night an enemy air-raid laid waste most of Keetons Road. The school was demolished by a 500lb bomb. Sidney Fagan's family home narrowly missed being destroyed when the house next door took a direct hit. Prefabs were later built on the bombed site. The houses have been pulled down since this 1976 photo. Plane trees, which annually shed their bark and with it London sooty grime, were planted in Keetons Road and surrounding areas at the instigation of Dr. Salter, and still line many streets of Bermondsey.

Coxson Place, south London, 1937. Families considered themselves fortunate if their homes boasted a tiny front garden. Most front doors opened onto the street from where visitors stepped straight into the living room. Back-to-back terrace houses did not even have the advantage of a back yard.

Where houses were in back-to-back terraces, toilets were sometimes in their own small blocks at the end of the terrace and it was a cold journey to make in winter so many families kept a bucket tucked away in the kitchen to save having to go out at night. In large tenement blocks such as Wolseley Buildings, Southwark, one lavatory near each stairwell did for as many as four families living on that landing and was not always kept in hygienic condition.

The Hair Cleansing and Disinfecting Station at Bermondsey (1937) was kept busy de-lousing children on a regular basis. Durbac soap or Lysol were used to kill the eggs and children were subjected to the misery of sitting over a newspaper for an hour or more while their hair was methodically checked through with a fine-toothed 'nit comb'.

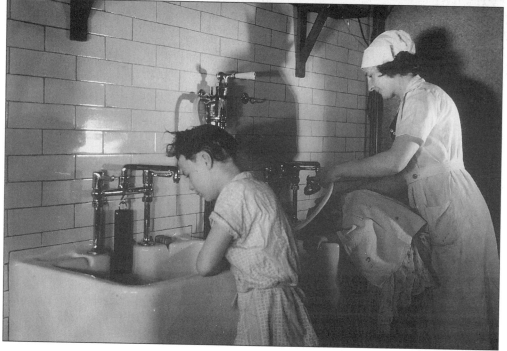

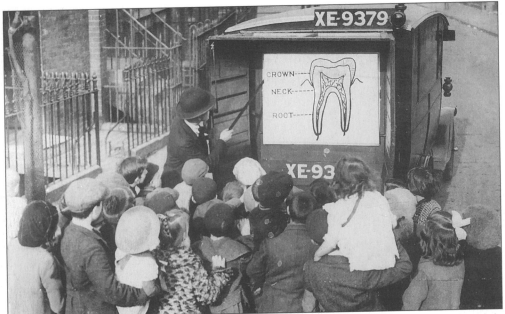

In an attempt to educate people to cleaner habits the Board of Health sent round mobile hygiene cinemas; small vans which opened up to reveal a shaded cinema screen around which families, particularly the children, gathered to watch films about an aspect of health care. This health officer in Bermondsey is showing how to care for the teeth.

The South Metropolitan Gasworks, Old Kent Road employed 3,000 women during World War One on light work previously considered unsuitable for females. The war took a heavy toll of able-bodied men and factories could only keep going by employing women for simple tasks. Then, '...recognising the women's adaptability (writes a contemporary south London paper about the Gas Board) decided to try them on other important work, and again they proved themselves equal to such tasks as attending gas engines, delivering coke... drilling and screwing machines and lathes...'

Machine factories were hot, noisy, dangerous and demanded long working hours. The women in Barrow and Hepburn's sewing factory are 'war workers', making leather bags and enjoyed unusually good working conditions, although the noise from all those sewing machines together with the music from *Worker's Playtime* must have been deafening: less fortunate machinists in other factories worked in dangerously cramped circumstances, their machines were poorly lit and the factories lacked decent basic amenities.

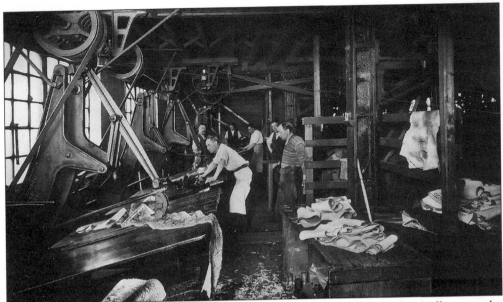

The specialist trade of skin polishing at Bevington's, June 1931. The leather mills covered a large area in Bermondsey, much of which was taken up by deep tanning pits used for soaking and curing the hides. The nauseating smell was overpowering to anyone new to Bermondsey and pervaded the surrounding houses. Leather was more widely used before the war than it is today. The tannery supplied hides for covering furniture, for coats, aprons, boots and shoes, bellows, shoes, harness, saddlery, luggage, bags, gaskets, washers and many articles now manufactured from synthetic materials.

Results of a bombing raid on Hampton's Avenue, south London. Some streets were completely devastated in a night, destroying many family homes and possessions. Victims had to do the best they could. This may mean taking up residence in the least-damaged houses already evacuated by families moving to a safer area or moving away to family and friends. Many children were evacuated to other parts of the country 'for the duration'(of the war).

The Blitz not only ruined people's homes, it took their jobs, too. This is all that was left of Hartley's Jam factory, once employing over 1000 workers, after nearby Surrey Commercial Docks were attacked in World War Two. While Hartley's kept on a small, permanent staff, employment was largely seasonal according to the intake of currently available fruit, so Bermondsey was treated to a variety of flavoursome aromas corresponding to the plums, strawberries, gooseberries or blackberries being processed.

What could be worse than losing your local pub where you usually met your friends to relax in the evenings after a hard day's work? Social, as well as home and working life, was disrupted during the Blitz. The Pitt's Head Public House at Bankside suffered bomb damage and had to be closed down. A father with nine children stands forlornly outside by the gaslamp.

The Admiral Hawke, damaged at the rear, carries on business regardless as these ladies pop in for their mid-day stout. Before the war it was common for children to be seen scurrying to the 'local' for a jug of ale or stout on behalf of an older family member: there was no 'under 18's' rule to prevent quite small children from being handed a pint or quart pot of brew, and many a surreptitious swig was taken on the way home.

Local corner shops were vital to the old neighbourhoods and the community spirit. This Swan Road, Bermondsey tobacconist sold a wide variety of goods including newspapers, as well as acting as the meeting point for a neighbourly chat, a place to leave messages for friends and source of the latest gossip. Local pride was strong. People were inclined to stay in their own area, even when they moved house. This helped foster a tight community spirit, a feeling of security and firm self-identity, something which is lost in today's transient population of temporary accommodation, high-rise flats and frequently- changed jobs.

An East End Market.

The cheapest way to buy food was in the markets, often open six days a week. Small stalls, many selling home-made or second-hand goods, offered life's necessities at reasonable prices. Second-hand stalls enabled impoverished families to afford essential furniture, plates and cutlery, prams and cast-off clothing. Children wore 'hand-me-downs', even footwear. Families relied on money earned hop-picking to buy new boots.

The EAST END SIEGE,
Scots Guards ready for the appearance of Assassins

The notorious Sidney Street siege in January, 1911 was controlled by over a thousand police and soldiers, including the Scots Guards, as the crowd surrounded the house in which three anarchists, suspected of murdering three policemen, were trapped. Two anarchists died later as the house burned down.

Many still have unhappy memories of the 1930's Depression following the Wall Street Crash, which caused a sharp drop in overseas trade and widespread unemployment even among highly skilled men. Unskilled jobs paid pittance wages. Innocently caught up in the complexities of world economics, many families were on the brink of starvation. There was general discontent. The London Dock strike drew a vast number of supporters for that extra sixpence wage ($2\frac{1}{2}$p today's value) and the dockers marched on Parliament to press their claim, causing consternation in the House. Unlike other strikes, their conduct was reasonably orderly judging by the few policemen required to control it.

Not all marchers protested silently and this early Black Maria, suitably pulled by black horses, and its stalwart 'Bobbies' were always ready to collect anyone who got out of line.

Hop farmers, pickers and workers were unable to earn a decent living in the 1940s because of an influx of cheap Continental hops. To safeguard their jobs, workers across north Kent united to demand the imposition of a tax on all foreign hops, hoping to stem the flow of imports. These workers come from east Peckham, Maidstone and Wincham.

These pickers travelled from Faversham and Canterbury to register their protest. At the back of the picture are dray horses delivering goods to nearby shops. The marchers are accompanied by a brass band. Notice how old and thin many of the men looked, yet most would only be in their thirties or forties.

'Pull no more bines!' Mr Harry Shepherd picked his last hop at Bluebell Hill Farm, Kent in 1986. The beginning of the end for hop-pickers came with the introduction of mechanization in the mid-1950s. By the late 1970s traditional hop-picking was a thing of the past and only a few farms continued the old tradition of hiring hand-pickers, mainly those unable to run to the expense of installing expensive machinery.

Once mechanization came into force farmers could strip a whole field of hops using only a handful of workers, rather than the small army previously required. Three or four workers, standing in special metal frames attached to the back of a truck could easily reach the overhead wires to cut the bines, tossing them into the truck bed in front of them. The load was then transported to the shed, fed into massive machines which stripped them of hops. A few workers were needed to pick out any debris such as leaves or stems, as the hops passed before them on a conveyor belt ready to be bagged.

Today, the noise and dust from modern machines contrasts sharply with formerly peaceful hopgardens where workers enjoyed the song of larks and other birds and the only other sounds were the calls from the binmen, tally clerks and workers, the soft clop of hooves in the dust, a distant lowing of cattle and happy cries of children glad to escape from the city's confines to the freedom of the countryside.

Modern Hoppers, in vastly reduced numbers, still return to the hopgardens of their youth with their families. Some keep caravans down on the farm, returning there each year. Others continue to use the old Hopper's huts. There is still a warm camaraderie among pickers but conversations are hard to keep up above mechanized clatter, so much of the banter and repartee has disappeared. Ex-Hoppers talk nostalgically of 'the happiest times in my childhood' eager to share family anecdotes of contented days in the perennial sunshine. Some have written their own hopping histories.

Hop-picking will never be the same, but the memories shown here are all happy ones and may raise a few reminiscences of your own.

Two
Maidstone, East and West Malling, Wateringbury

The Maidstone area includes East and West Malling, Otham, Wateringbury and surrounding districts. It was the easiest to reach for those hoppers relying on their own transport from London. All manner of transport was pressed into use: the rag-and-bone man's horse and cart, market carts, vans, lorries. Some lorry owners were glad to supplement their income by taking five or six families down to the hop gardens in one journey, all piled onto the back with their belongings.

Stella, Mum and Rodney Ash rest at one of the Bins in the hop-field at May's Farm, West Malling in 1950. Leaning against one of the poles is Phyllis Ash's old bike, used to cycle two miles into the village for any necessary shopping or to post postcards home to family and friends.

Stella, Reggie, Brenda and Rodney Ash at May's farm. Even the dog went with them. '…everything but the kitchen sink, and even that went, sometimes.' Because there was no-one left at home to look after any pets -even the neighbours would be at the hop gardens- hoppers brought their pets with them, whether it be a cat, canary, budgie or dog.

Rod Ash outside their hut, No. 31. The Ash's lived here up to six weeks, including a few days preparing the hut for use, four to five weeks hop-picking, according to the abundance of the crop, plus a day or two to clear up, afterwards. The hut, housing the whole family, consisted of one windowless room.

Some years the hop crop was abundant and this meant a good return for their labour. There was always time for a laugh while the picking was in progress. Mrs Lovell and family enjoy a joke between sessions of hard work.

Long wood-and-canvas bins were located at the end of each hop row. Hops had to be stripped cleanly, leaving no leaves or stalks attached. Any 'extras' which got into the bin were usually pushed down out of sight by the pickers. Bins were portable and were lifted by wooden handles from the end of a stripped row on to the next row to be picked.

The hop cart was always on the go, being filled with pokes (long sacks filled by with hops from the bins) to be transported to the oasts, then back to the gardens ready for the next load. Rod Ash has been lucky to get a ride.

Two pretty hoppers stripping the bines at Mays Farm, W. Malling were Phyllis Ash's mother and friend, keeping an eye on the photographer in 1951. After working in the fields all day, the evenings were for socialising. Sing-songs, dances and barbecues were popular and the young pickers made the most of these opportunities to meet members of the opposite sex.

Newly arrived at the hop garden in 1952, pickers were dressed for their holiday. Once they began work they changed to old clothes to preserve their 'best'. The Ash family picked regularly at May's Farm in West Malling.

Sometimes there was an opportunity for children to escape from hop-picking for a while and do a bit of exploring in the surrounding countryside. Ten-year-old Rodney Ash visited the ruins of an eighteenth century castle near the farm.

Joan and Winnie Hope working hard at filling the bins assisted by a friend, 1951. The days were often hot, there was little shade except from a hat or any bines still strung. The work was rough on hands as the scratchy hops needed a firm pull to release them from the bine, particularly if the bine had gone a bit soft. Fingers became stained with the juice which stung any cuts as it contained beta acid. Some pickers developed hop dermatitis. In order to get their hops to market quickly to make the best prices, farmers started their pickers at first light, continuing until sunset except for short breaks for lunch, morning and afternoon teas, so the day was long as well as hot.

A hop farm at the beginning of the twentieth century. The hop poles are shorter than usual on this farm. It must have been very uncomfortable for the ladies in their long dresses. Children wore 'pinnies' to protect their clothes from tears and staining and, unlike the 1950s, everyone wore hats to shade from the sun. A loosely-filled poke lies in the foreground, while in the left background a lady in dark dress can be seen holding open a poke being filled by the bearded man using a bushel basket. In the centre of the picture an overseer is directing work.

K. Harrison's family were regular pickers and the whole family, from great- grandmother to great-grand children, would travel down annually to Fremlin's Farm at Nettlesham, Wateringbury.

There had to be time for children to play and here two little Harrisons have 'hopped' into one of the bins. It is doubtful if they stayed there long as hops make an uncomfortable bed unless enclosed in protective material.

The Harrison's were fortunate to be provided with a brick purpose-built hut, There was no glass in the door window. Instead, it had a wooden shutter to close on chilly nights. The seven Harrison children pose with their parents for a family photo.

Mr Harrison appreciates a moment of relaxation at the end of a long day.

Kath Embleton with a bucket of water ready-heated on a wood fire for the family's evening wash. In the background is the family table brought down specially from home. Above it is the wooden box 'larder' to keep milk and butter cool. There were no refrigerators.

By the 1950s hop farmers no longer required an army of pickers to harvest their crops. With advances in technology, hop-picking gradually became mechanized and a valuable source of income was denied to the willing fingers of their former work-forces who then became redundant.

HOPPING HOLIDAY 17 8 64

ABOUT 10,000 Londoners from Bow, Stepney, Bermondsey and Rotherhithe are preparing for their annual September holiday in the Kent hopfields.

They are a vanishing race; hop - picking machines increase in number each year and this autumn it is estimated that at least 70 per cent of the crop will be machine-picked.

Before the last war, the number of Londoners clearing the bines would have been closer to 80,000.

It used to be possible for an East-End family to have a holiday picking hops and also return home with £20 or £30 in their pockets. But things have changed since then and most pickers settle for just a working holiday paid for by the hops.

Board Water Farm, East Malling, 1952. Working at the bins. In the background can be seen pokes being loaded onto a lorry.

A team of pole pullers and bin men on Board Water Farm, East Malling, 1947. Because of their long working hours, often in poor working conditions, labourers tended to look older than their years, so the oldest may be in his early fifties, while the youngest around mid-teens. The pole held by the third man from the right is a bine hook, topped by a curved knife used to cut and hook down bines caught at the top of the wires.

Apparently you are never too old to go hopping. Here Joe and Edieth Scott are still going strong although both are over 80 years of age. In an age when families looked after their own and it was unthinkable to put grandma or grandpa into a 'home', wherever the family went, so did Grandma and Grandpa. The threat of being put into the dreaded workhouse by 'the authorities' lasted well beyond the life of such institutions. As late as the 1950s it was common to hear old people speak uneasily of 'the poorhouse', and of their care in saving enough money to pay for their own respectable funeral.

Board Water Farm, 1954. The faster pickers could strip the bines, the quicker they filled their bins. At the end of the day it was the number of bushels per family that counted. This young picker is so practiced that the speed of her fingers outwit the camera.

The Baker family of Rotherhithe at
Bell Common, Paddock Wood,
c. 1940.

Not everyone could manage two months' work in the hopfields, and these 1930s elegantly-dressed ladies are ready to be taken by charabanc on a day's outing to the hop gardens from the Princess Alexandra pub (otherwise known as the 'Cocko-Money'). On arrival at the fields they would be expected to pay the traditional 'footshoes', or dues. In exchange they could step in, or have their shoes rubbed with hops before entering the fields and would be invited to that evening's celebration.

It was difficult to keep an eye on babies when on the job, there was so much mischief they could get into as well as carelessly-laid knives, sharp, discarded bines and nearby ditches. Watching baby meant less attention and speed in picking so, while this cartoon is making fun of the women's use of vocabulary, it also helps to highlight one of their main problems.

Three
Mr Duncan Bennock's Collection

Mr Bennock accumulated a collection of Hopping postcards and other memorabilia, of which he has allowed us to use a selection. The end of the nineteenth and beginning of the twentieth centuries was the hey-day for picture postcards. Even as late as 1950 it only cost 2½d (just over 1p) to send a postcard anywhere in the British Isles. Picture postcards were popular with Hoppers, who sent them to their friends to tell them about their country holiday.

Faversham, c. 1935 During the week pickers were mainly women and children. The men would continue their normal work through the week, only going to the hopfields for weekends.

A happy group posing for one of the professional photographers who toured the hopfields, annually, photographing anyone who could afford their services.

A set of pickers at the beginning of the century.

Hop bines were planted in rows with alleys between to allow room for tending. Hop 'sets' or roots were grown on individual 'hills' and lasted more than one season. They required much time-consuming care in the early stages of growth: hoeing, trimming, removing pipey stems, dusting with fungicide and 'twiddling.' Each tendril was carefully twiddled, or trained around one of the vertical strings attached to horizontal overhead wires. This healthy crop would be viewed with delight by the pickers. Well-filled bines ensured a good return at the end of a season.

Hop-picking at Chilham, Kent. The tallyman is notching up this family's work before handing over a metal token which would be changed for cash at the end of the season.

General views of the gardens showing loading up the poke wagon with hop-filled pokes; a nearly-completed hop garden with a now-rare square oast house in the background; the final stage of the pockets being delivered and a well-ordered pickers' camp.

A group of Edwardian pickers working by the bins. The clothes of the day must have been most uncomfortable in the hot sun. Each bine has been cut and removed together with its pole for easier plucking. Considering the unmade state of many Kent roads, nineteenth century pickers would be grateful for the introduction of the railway to the area. The trains' hard, wooden seats were better and quicker than travelling by horse and cart or walking.

Whitbreads Brewery owned one of the best kept, larger hop gardens. Pickers were well paid and lived in comfortable quarters. With eighteen oasts to keep in production there was plenty of work for those lucky to be taken on. The majority of hoppers returned to the same farms annually. If employers were too meagre with pay and facilities, pickers moved on to other farms.

Hop pokes being unloaded for drying in the oasts at Whitbreads, Paddock Wood. These buildings and the magnificent shire horses used for pulling the carts can be seen today by visitors to the Farm. Nostalgic ex-pickers can walk round a life-like exhibition depicting the arrival of pickers at Paddock Wood by train, through all the stages of hop-growing to final delivery.

Drifts (organised groups) of pickers worked their way in orderly fashion across the hop fields, moving from one row to the next after completion. Two drifts of mothers and children are finishing the last of their bines in one field, while the quicker, mainly adult pickers have already moved on to the next.

Carefully-stacked hop pockets being loaded for a Yorkshire brewery, ready for carting to the station. The horses are being fed a mixture of corn and chaff in their sacking nosebags while they wait. Hop pockets were heavy, and this was young men's work.

Hop Pickers loading on Rail

Railway wagons being loaded with hop pockets straight from a farm cart. Each pocket was clearly labelled with the year as a guarantee to brewers that the hops were the new seasons, and not left-overs from a previous year.

Green (undried) hops being carted from the fields to be roasted in the kilns of these more unusual square oast houses in Kent.

49

Kent Pole Tug 1967

A Kent pole tug, used for transporting and collecting the heavy, cumbersome poles along the aisles ready to be erected ready for the sprouting bines. Early poles were usually of durable alder, particularly in damp soil where they were likely to rot at the base. Metal poles came into use at a later date. Poles were about 25ft high

Whitbreads ran a series of colourful Inn signs cards featuring pub names, given free with their products. 'The Hop Pole' was a favoured name for pubs across Kent. The village pub was popular as a meeting place for both men and women hoppers after a day in the fields as they gathered for reminiscences, a sing-song and a few pints.

September saw droves of gipsy families taking their vardos, or horse-drawn caravans, to the gardens. They sometimes supplemented their income by catching rabbits and selling them on to Hopping families for their evening meals. Hoppers were ready customers for the woven baskets, wooden clothes pegs and other goods peddled by the gypsies. The gypsies provided traditional remedies for ailments. They knew that hops, considered a safe herb, contain natural bacteria-killing chemicals which help combat infection and were useful in their range of natural medicines. Dried hops are an aid to digestion and act as a sedative. The late, respected Romany, Leon Petulengro, suggested insomnia could easily be avoided by taking short, brisk walks late at night before sleeping on a hop-filled pillow.

Picture postcards were a popular mode of correspondence, being cheap to buy and cheap to post. Doris and family were hopping in the Maidstone area when she dutifully wrote to keep in touch with her grandmother.

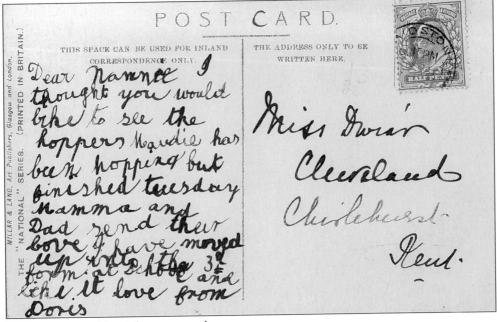

Reverse, written side of above postcard

Mr Prosser sent a series of picture postcards to his young lady from Chilham. He writes 'This is the floor where the hops are put to cool previous to being pocketed you will observe the press that puts the hops in the pockets. With kind regards' He signs it formally 'A. Brian Prosser.'

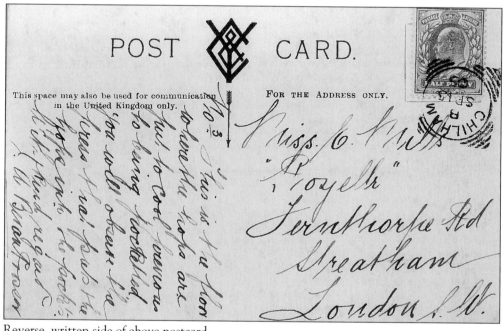

Reverse, written side of above postcard

Kent Oast Houses

Oast houses are picturesque as well as useful. The grace of these long-gone oasts contributed to Kent's reputation of beauty as 'The Garden of England' and stirred many a hopper's heart on the initial ride down from smoky London.

Four
The Weald

The North Weald is one of Kent's most beautiful areas, popular nowadays with hikers and ramblers who appreciate the largely unspoilt countryside. At the beginning of the twentieth century this part of Kent was well-known for its hopfields and apple orchards. Now, much of the land has been turned over to dairy and crop farming. Swathes of acid-yellow rape fields carpet the hillsides and many of the hedges and walls have been removed to make larger fields for easier use of the tractor.

Pickers at the end of the day, Paddock Wood.

Mrs Hull, her sister Carrie and their daughters went regularly to Fowle Hall Farm, Paddock Wood. They continued after World War Two. Behind them on the right of the picture are their huts, and the toilets are in the building to the left.

Mrs Hull's daughters enjoyed sitting on the tractor being loaded with hop pokes at Fowle Hall Farm, Paddock Wood. 1946.

The Salvation Army regularly travelled down to hopping villages. As well as singing cheerful hymns and carrying The Word of the Lord to hoppers they offered practical help. Brigadier L. Daw and Lt. Col. E. Four Acre, two leaders from London, visited Beltring Church in 1952, ready to conduct a service there.

The hopper's day started early. Here, Captain Pat Skinner (Chaplain) and fellow Salvation Army member prepare tea at six-thirty in the morning ready to serve pickers before they set off for the fields.

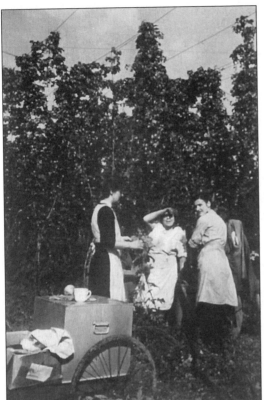

Officers of the 'Sally Army', as it was affectionately known, travelled down from Shadwell Goodwill Centre, London with officers from Deptford, Bethnal Green and Notting Hill to help in the hopgardens at Beltring and Goudhurst. Taking it in turns, officers rose at 0630 to brew tea and push it to the gardens. Tea and cakes were served free to the pickers who were glad to stop for a chat and a break. Captain Pat Skinner (now Mrs Boyce) enjoyed the chance to get to know the Beltring workers better.

The Canadian branch of the Salvation Army sent a mobile 'Canteenette' to the London Salvation Army to help them serve free teas. It was decided to take it down to Beltring but proved impossibly heavy and the ladies couldn't push it through the mud.

It wasn't only the humans the Salvation Army cared for. Chaplain Pat Skinner felt it was the hop-cart horse's turn to receive a tit-bit. Salvation Army officers also helped out at the hoppers' doctor's surgery. They wore long buff-colour aprons embroidered with 'Goodwill'. For six weeks they lived in white-washed hoppers huts on the farm. Saturday evening religious meetings were held outside 'The Vine', Goudhurst.

Ken Higgs and his family were regular hoppers and worked as a team on their own drift.

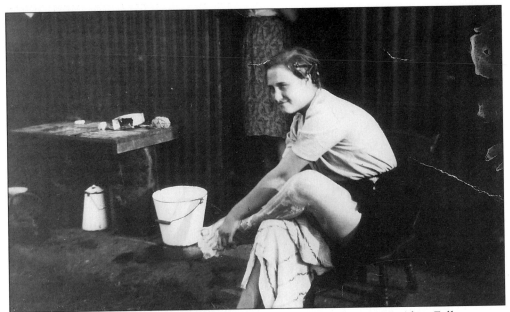

The Fullerton family worked at Bell Common, Paddock Wood in 1949. Alice Fullerton was glad to sit outside their hut and wash the dust off her feet at the end of the day. Alice still has metal curlers in her hair, ready to style it for an evening out.

Robert and Mrs Hepzibah Slater and family (John, Robert jnr with father and, front row, Rene, Sam and Eliza, in hat) Aparacio picked on Mercers Farm at Headcorn in 1927. There was a real sense of achievement in completing one row of hops, ready to move on to the next. Everyone was expected to do their share of the work. In 1995 Hepzibah was 97 years old.

Mr Slater sometimes took the family down to the nearby river in their free time.

Sam Aparacio snr and jnr, and Robert Slater snr are ready for dinner. In the distance are oast houses, picker's huts and an infant playing happily on its own outside the huts.

Mrs Skinner enjoying a well-earned cup of tea with her family. A wooden box has proved useful as a table. Cloche hats were popular in the 1930s and gave good service as sun hats, too.

World War One and World War Two interrupted the business of hop-picking. Men were away fighting and women worked in munitions factories or did other essential war work. Still, hop-picking and beer-making were considered essential to the War Effort as morale boosters. Men home on leave looked forward to a pint or too, and it made a pleasant break to go down hopping with the family, even if only for a day's outing. Aircraftsman Arthur Ellis and relatives went to Pembles Farm in Paddock Wood.

Alan Turpin's family: William and Florence Turpin, John Wright and children Geoffrey Wright, Sylvia Turpin and Linda Wright at Chittenden Farm, Staplehurst in 1963.

The wartime order to civilians was that gasmasks were to be carried at all times, wherever they went. It seemed inconceivable that anyone could be in any danger in the middle of a Kentish hopfield but these 1940 pickers complied with the order, nevertheless. Farms were occasionally under attack by enemy aircraft when pilots released their bombs indiscriminately instead of on a city target and sometimes hoppers were fired on from the air.

Victorian pickers stripping the bines, which have been plucked together with their poles and laid behind the pickers. With this method, one end of each pole was laid across the horizontal wooden bar across the bin, which made the bines easier to deal with as the hops were more accessible. The postcard was sent in 1908 to Miss T. Wallace, c/o Capt. Ismay at Blackheath.

George Shrieve's Uncle Jim Edmonds and Nan peeling potatoes and trimming beans for the evening meal. An iron cooking pot stands ready on the table outside their hut at East Malling.

Mrs A. M. Hull's son Terry, daughter Joan and sister's son John West and daughter Rita at Fowle Hall Farm, Paddock Wood just after the war. Terry was a reluctant hop-picker, and not even willing to pretend for the photograph. The family transported their belongings by van including tables, chairs and proper beds rather than sleep on straw mattresses. They painted and papered the hut walls to make it homely. Mrs Hull was proud to have modern conveniences such as a Primus stove and Tilley lamp. Mr Hull came down at weekends, as did a host of visitors.

The Fullerton family at Bell Common, Paddock Wood, enjoying a ride in the hopfarm cart in 1949.

The family of F. Wood picked at a farm at Marden in 1946. This looks to be a particularly healthy crop, so their takings could have be in the region of £30 to £35 at the end of the season. Experienced Hoppers travelling to their garden from home looked keenly at the state of the hops along their route: a weedy crop meant poor pickings for the season.

F. Woods and family at the end of a hop aisle. The man in an apron holds a hop pole, ready to hook down the bines.

Tired at the end of their first day's picking . Mrs D. Farman (mother), grandmother, brother and Joyce had left home at 5 o'clock in the morning to catch the first train from West Norwood to reach William Day's Farm, Marden in time for the start of picking.

George Thirkell outside the family hut. The watering can was used to transport water from a nearby tap for drinking, washing and cooking. An enamel jug and basin are ready for ablutions. The snake 'S' elastic belt George is wearing was popular with children in the 1950s. Hooks on the back of the only door came in handy as a makeshift wardrobe. Corrugated iron huts were stiflingly hot on sunny days and chilly on cold nights.

Among the pickers at Chittenden Farm, Staplehurst were Alan Turpin's family. Mrs Turpin still had to look after the youngest infant while filling the bins from the bines.

Too hot for a coat. Mrs Reeve hangs hers on a handy pole at the end of the bin while she gets on with the job at Horsemonden.

Lunch was a picnic beside the bins. Pauline Mayern's family had to prepare sandwiches the previous night, because there would be no time before the morning start.

72

The Mayern family was sufficiently large to make up a set of their own. Pickers were expected to leave their picnic site tidy after the meal, so any rubbish had to be cleared straight away once they had finished eating.

Time for a sitdown and a cuppa. The Mayern family have just finished stripping their row and are ready for a break.

Mrs D. Simmons with her aunt and Mrs Ballard of Swanley Lane at Maplesome Farm, Natts Valley near Farningham, busy at the bins.

Time for Mr F.J. Jex to indulge in a wash and brush up after a dusty day in Whitbreads gardens.

Mr and Mrs Jex and several generations of their family prepare the evening meal outside their hut. A mirror and clothes hang on the back of the open door, while a frying pan, and even a picture, hang on handy nails knocked into wooden supports of the corrugated iron walls.

Gran Shrieve sitting under the family's tin bath hanging on the wall. This kind of bath was in common use in tenements and houses where there was no bathroom. The table is nicely laid with a cloth ready for the evening meal, 1936.

The day's picking may be over but there was still work to be done. Everyone, including the children, was expected to help with the chores, even after a long day in the fields. There was washing to hang out, firewood to collect and potatoes to peel for dinner. These 1946 hopping huts were nicknamed 'Rat's Castle' (after the rodents found in nearby fields) at The Common, Paddock Wood.

Mum and Gran Shrieve with their pile of firewood outside hut No.1. Behind them are Cousin Kath and Mrs Widders who had come down to visit for the day.

The Shrieves getting ready to go home in 1949. The young lad is holding a driving whip for a horse cart. Mrs Shrieve is unravelling twine ready to tie up their belongings, while Mr Shrieve is fastening things onto the packing-case handcart which runs on four pram wheels and would have come down with them from home.

Sidney Cave's step-father, Mother Alice and stepsister Doris, little Alfie Masters and Sidney, aged eight years at their regular farm, W.T. Tompsett, Park Farm near Horsmonden in 1935. They, and three or four other families, travelled by lorry from London. Twice a week Halls, bakers from New Cross, travelled down to the hop huts to sell cakes and bread. Mr Frost was a Pole Puller, while little Sidney was a Sack Distributor as well as hop-picker for their set. A set comprised twelve-fourteen people. Mr Frost supplemented his earnings by making toffee apples and sweets in the evenings. Sidney was sent round the huts to sell them but was not allowed to eat any until later.

Five

Mr Sidney Perrier's Private Collection, 1906

Born in 1888 at South Norwood, Mr Perrier contracted tuberculosis at eighteen and as part of his convalescence was sent to the hopfields of Paddock Wood. As a keen photographer, he took the opportunity to record the sights, and even managed to stage some 'set pieces' such as his pictures of 'The Cake Walk'. He died in 1948 when his illness returned. Titles in inverted commas are Mr Perrier's own captions to each picture.

A group of hop-pickers near Paddock Wood.

'A slight altercation'. The onlookers look so cheerful that at worst this fight was a 'friendly', with no harm done.

'Set 31'. A set of pickers. The infant is wearing a home-made sun bonnet, while the ladies have protected their clothing with hop-sacking.

'Set 28' was a larger group, ranging from infants to great grandfather.

'A Family of Pickers'. This is a revealing picture of the dress at the end of the nineteenth century. The man wears corduroy trousers tied below the knee with string, as was common among farm workers in the countryside at that time to keep out small rodents and avoid trouser legs getting in the way of sharp sickles or scythes. The lady wears her Edwardian boater, the eldest boy is in knickerbocker trousers with a jerkin over his shirt, the middle boy in a sailor suit and bare feet while the smaller boy wears hand-me-downs with boots. The pretty little girl is also wearing boots. Their picnic lunch waits nearby in a basket.

'Measuring'. The measurer checks to see that each bushel basketful taken from the bin consists only of hops, and that bulk has not been added with leaves, stems or bits of bines.

Measurers filling the pokes from bushel baskets ready to transport them to the oasts. Bine pullers were expected to help measurers lifting the pokes onto carts and drive them to the stores ready for drying.

'Dinner time: Leaving Work'. At the end of the day, the boss called 'Pull no more bines', which was the signal for pickers to stop work, leave their bins tidy, pack up their belongings, including lunch baskets or boxes and return to their huts for their evening meal, yet to be prepared.

'Leaving the Hop Garden'. Some workers had walks of two or three miles from their hopfield back to the huts. There were no buses. These ladies are still wearing their hopsack aprons, while one girl seems to have trouble with scratches itching on her leg. One treat the hoppers enjoyed was walking down to the local village shops or pub, while the children enjoyed running on the village green.

'Gipsy Lea: King of the Gypsies'. Lea is a true Romany name. By tradition a King and Queen are picked from among the oldest Romany families in the area. Gipsy Lea has been accorded a chair in keeping with his proud position, and picks his hops directly into a tin bath, possibly for separate measuring, rather than into the communal bin behind him.

'The Cake Walk, by Hop-Pickers'. The Cake walk was a popular fun-fair and Music Hall item. These likely young men have entered into the spirit of it cheerfully enough to oblige Mr Perrier and his camera. The fun-fair 'Cake Walk' consisted of an unstable, slatted footway which moved in all directions and on which it was very difficult to keep ones balance even if holding onto the handrails. The Music Hall dance routine developed from this.

Six

Faversham, Canterbury and West Kent

Most hop gardens have gone from around the West Kent area now. Some farmers still grow hops, though the process is nearly all mechanized. Modern methods are noisy, require large machinery and fewer workers. Old pickers miss the socialising of former hand-gathered hop methods. Today's Hoppers take their own caravans to provide accommodation on the farms, using the old hopping huts for storage or for sleeping quarters for some members of the family. Faversham has a country museum where displays of hop-picking memorabilia are shown.

Three generations of the Kennard family cook their evening meal at Brendley Farm, Faversham in 1933. The family first went hopping in 1921. The heavy iron cooking pots were ideal for camp fires as they returned the heat with less chance of burning the contents. The pot's handles were of hollow iron tubing and the lids are of 'tinanimal' (enamelled-tin).

Some farmers provided barbecue-style cooking fireplaces for their pickers, but most left them to furnish their own. Mrs G.E. Mason's family made do with a circle of bricks to support their cooking pots and pans as dad shares out the fried sausages. Behind them is their supply of firewood.

The Mason family rest outside their huts after work. 1951. Mrs Mason's young brother caught the vaguely-named 'hop germ' and became so ill he required two operations, one on his hand and a second on his leg. Fortunately he recovered, but by then the family felt it was best not to go again, despite enjoying hopping.

Working in the fields often gave fathers their best opportunity to get to know their children better. A normal working week for a labourer could be from seven or eight o'clock in the morning until six at night. This often meant that by the time they reached home the younger children were already in bed and asleep. As a child Mrs A. Lovell enjoyed a day's work in the company of her father at Brogdale, Ospringe.

Bulltown Farm, Brabourne near Ashford grew the last hops in the Brabourne area. Mrs Chittenden's grandparents, Harry and Harriet Edwards and family picked here over the 1900 to 1914 seasons.

Sometimes their 'local' arranged a day's hop-picking for customers, travelling in style in a charabanc (early twentieth century) or coach. These ladies enjoyed their day out from the Shipwright Arms, Chatham in 1949.

The Riley family's hut at Faversham was in the 'luxury' class compared to most pickers' accommodation. They were not only built on a raised brick plinth, but also boasted glazed, shuttered windows. A 1930s-style perambulator can be seen behind the oldest boy.

A happy group from the Shipwright Arms, Chatham, 1949, out for a day's picking and pocket money. The elderly lady at the right is wearing a dress fashionable for the times.

Casually dressed to suit the hot weather, Mrs Riley carries her enamel bucket to the water tap before making their evening meal.

Mrs Vasallo from Medway Towns, taking a brief rest after filling a bushel basket during six weeks hopping at Brendley Farm, near Faversham in 1935. Six bushel baskets made up one tally basket, so there was a lot of work to do before earning each token from the tallyman.

Mr and Mrs Fieldhouse with children and grandchildren at Brendley Farm, Faversham, owned by Major Barry, 1935. Mrs E. Diddell's aunt, Eileen Phillips, ready to make the breakfast porridge. Grandpa Fieldhouse stands behind Mrs Diddell (aged ten), Grandma Fieldhouse is in the deckchair. Mrs Fieldhouse has put up the usual 'privacy curtain' and also a net curtain (of cotton lace) at the windowless opening. The door would have been left open most of the time, especially on hot summer nights, so the privacy curtain was a necessity.

The Fieldhouse girls pose beside the Brendley Farm cumbersome water carrier used to provide fresh water for the pickers. It had to be hauled to the farmyard, filled with water, and pulled back to near the hoppers' huts; a heavy task after a full day's work.

Baby Riley kept away from mischief in a bath tub filled with hops. 1953.

Square oast house at Faversham. The earliest oast kilns used charcoal to heat their furnaces. Modern kilns are powered by oil-fired heating.

At the beginning of the twentieth century Mrs Q. Garrett's mother, Mrs Ford, had thirteen children, eleven of which survived. A widow, Mrs Ford and children were regular hoppers at a farm outside Sandwich to supplement their meagre income. They travelled there by horse and cart. These three little girls, wearing leather lace-up boots paid for out of their hopping earnings, are well in their eighties at the time this book is printed. Mrs Ford wore her best hat for the visiting photographer.

Ron Riley took his dog to their Faversham farm. Farmers were strict about animals and dogs were not always allowed into the hop garden so were kept chained at the huts.

Post-war pickers at Faversham. Janet, Mum, friend, son Barry, Norma and Len Riley in 1951.

The smallest Rileys found a young rabbit to play with while waiting for dinner.

'Oh, my aching feet!' The Rileys finishing off the last of a row.

Mrs Riley washing the clothes using an old army canteen as a bowl. On the ground is the tin bath while behind are two bushel hop baskets.

The Riley family dressed and packed ready to go home at the end of the season. Faversham, 1953.

The Mayern family eating sandwich 'doorsteps' and fresh fruit with their tea.

Lunch time at Bekesbourne Hopgardens in the 1930s.

Mr Lovell lights his primus stove to boil up the urn ready for a lunch-time cup of tea. The bines are nearly all stripped, so their holiday at Brogdale Farm, near Ospringe is nearly over.

There is more than one way to string a hop garden. These bines are strung across to the adjacent row, instead of straight up their own pole in *Butcher's Vinery* method' of 1875. Bines were also cross-strung, alternately from left to right across the aisle, in an 'umbrella' setup, or the American system. Other methods were preferred in different parts of the country.

Isn't it difficult when you've just dropped something into an almost-empty bin and you have to fish to the bottom to get it out ? An amusing predicament at Whitbread's Hop Farm from the Jex family album.

Seven
Tools of the Trade

All these tools and implements would have been very familiar to the old hop-pickers. The only tools pickers required were nimble fingers, but regular farm workers who trained and dusted, watered and tended their hops throughout the year needed special tools to do the job, such as the hop dog, used to grub up the poles supporting the bine stringing. As well, there were pokes and the larger pockets used to contain the hops, tokens used to pay hoppers until their final day at the gardens when tokens were exchanged for money. They were all part and parcel of the romance of the bygone trade of hand hop-picking.

Bellingham, Maidstone Samplers. The man second from the left uses a double- bladed knife for sampling the season's hops, while the man third from the right uses a single- bladed knife. Both knives are specially for the purpose. Each tightly-packed sample is carefully wrapped and labelled with the year it was packed (1895) then sent to the brewers for assessment. A rectangular printing block and 'pounce' (leather bag used for banging the back of the printing block to mark each parcel) can be seen with the already-packed samples, front right of the picture.

Poke-loading is hefty work and these men deserved their break for a beer at Robert Boucher's farm in 1952. 'Poke' is an ancient name for a sack. The saying 'To buy a pig in a poke', suggests that if you were asked to buy a pig (or anything else)- unseen, tied up in a sack, the seller's honesty is in doubt. Pokes were filled from bins, taken to oast houses, then packed tightly into pockets by a mechanical ram. Before the ram was invented, a Bagster stood in the poke, treading down until the hops were firm.

Fred Holtum and friend, carrying a ten bushel poke (approx. 360 litres.) up from the truck to the oast where they would be put in the hop store ready to be laid out on the overhead drying floors.

George Thirkell easily lifts the last poke out of the wagon at the end of the day. Sacks were tied at the neck with binding twine to prevent spillage.

Back-breaking work at the end of the day: Fred Holtum and others lifting pokes onto the storage floor of the Oast House.

Fred Holtum emptying a bushel basket into the measuring bin. Each darker ring of canework denoted approximately one bushel.

George Shrieve's family having their hops measured by the Measurer in 1952.

Now the Museum of Kent Life, these oasts are still used annually to roast hops grown in the Garden in the traditional manner.

Hops on the bine. Not a luxuriant crop, but plentiful enough to provide good pickings and returns for the pickers. Many problems contributed to poor crops in a season. Wilt was caused by a virus which, once in the soil, was nearly impossible to eradicate. Various blights were treated with a dusting of sulphur. Drought is an added difficulty for the farmer.

As any specialist trade, hopping developed implements and tools most suitable to do the work efficiently. The binmen's hooks were attached to a long shaft and were used to cut and hook down the bines ready to supply the pickers. Binmen were only allowed to help strip the bines if their own work was not being held up, and usually at the boss's discretion.

A Hop Dog —

④

The Gift of L. Slaughter Esq. O.B.E.
Egerton. —   November 1938.

A 1 5   Cms

Mr L. Slaughter, OBE, donated a 1938 Hop Dog in good condition to the Kent Museum for Rural Life. Hop dogs were used to grub up hop poles to creosote and store ready for the next season.

Each job required its own tool. Sampling was carried out by experts using purpose-made single or double-bladed knives kept razor sharp. Samplers had their personal preferences, but single blades were more popular, being easier to handle, although they needed four thrusts; double blades only required two thrusts but were cumbersome to use. The knives were made by local blacksmiths, sometimes to the design of the purchaser.

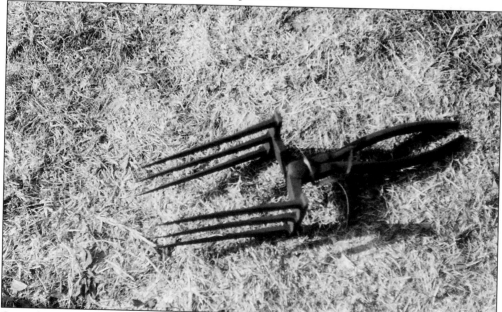

Once the sample had been cut from the tightly-packed hop pocket special tongs were needed to extract the sample, which was then wrapped and labelled with the farm, date, batch and hop-pocket number. Brewers relied on consistency of quality from hop suppliers, so sampling was essential: carelessly pressed pokes may develop 'slack pockets' where excessive moisture quickly turned surrounding hops mouldy, rendering them useless.

Not only men were poke-carriers. During the First World War women were needed to do mens' work while the men were at war. The young lady seems quite capable of lifting the poke from the cart to the oast storehouse. She is wearing canvas gaiters to protect her legs from scratches and for modesty's sake.

It was important to string the poles correctly at the beginning of the season. Loose strings gave poor support to the bines. With his bag of raffia or coir strings, a worker checks each string, repairing or replacing as necessary.

Tying strings to pole tops required men to reach up around 25ft, according to pole height. Stilts were found to be the best method and stiltwalkers were to be seen with bundles of raffia or string dangling from their belts, striding along the rows to secure each bine in place. However, stilts were twelve to thirteen feet high. In order to mount them, a stiltman had to first climb a ladder leaning against one of the poles.

Once up the ladder, the stiltman then had to set his feet on the footrest on each stilt before being strapped in at the feet and secured to the stilts by leather loops attached round his waist by a belt. It was a precarious job and required strong nerves until the stiltman got used to the height, and vulnerability of uneven ground, boggy places after wet weather, or dust pockets in the soil.

Stilts were originally of wood, but these were superseded by hollow metal stilts which were lighter to move and carry, and more manoeuvrable. Coir strings hang from his belt and he wears gloves, both to make it easier to grip the strings, and because if he slipped, the strong strings would cut his hands unless they were protected.

Stringing sacking to protect vulnerable bines required the help of stiltwalkers. This man balances easily on his wooden stilts while attaching hessian netting to a top wire, although a long length of hessian such as this must have been difficult to work with and not easy to keep steady.

The 'privvy' was usually close to the picker's huts. Sometimes they were well appointed, others were enclosed and roofed with corrugated iron which would have been very hot in the summer. A wooden seat and wood box covering surrounded a simple bucket which had to be emptied regularly by the Hoppers.

The Hop Marketing Board arranged for 'Hopper's Special's' with the Kent and East Sussex Railway. Boarding the trains at specified stops beginning with London Bridge, Hoppers could purchase a cheap fare ticket to the railway station nearest their hopgarden. Some Hoppers had to walk five or six miles from the train to their destination, pushing their handcart and contents.

The tallyman not only notched up a family's tally of full bins on their own tallystick, using a metal file or sharp knife strung from his collection of tallysticks. He was also responsible for issuing hop tokens to pickers as a token of the amount they were picked. When the Season was ended, tokens were handed in to the paymaster or farmer, who paid workers according to their reckoning.

Each farm had their own hop tokens. Sometimes these were merely stamped with the name of the farmer, others included the farm's address, date, and the number of bushels.

Hop tokens were often single-sided, of stamped tin. Others were more substantial and bore more resemblance to coins, being of more durable base metal and printed on both sides.

The obverse sides of the three tokens in the top picture show the amount of bushels they each represent. The top token is printed with a hop flower. The bottom left token shows two oast houses while the bottom right token pictures a hop poke.

Hop tokens are an old form of receipt for work done. No money changed hands until the end of the season. Instead, the tally man 'notched up' for each bushel picked per family and gave them a metal hop token as a reimbursement guarantee to be cashed in when the picking was done. These tokens are now prized, collectable items as is this token from the hop garden of Edmund Barham at Doleham farm, Westfield, who were issuing tokens in 1855.

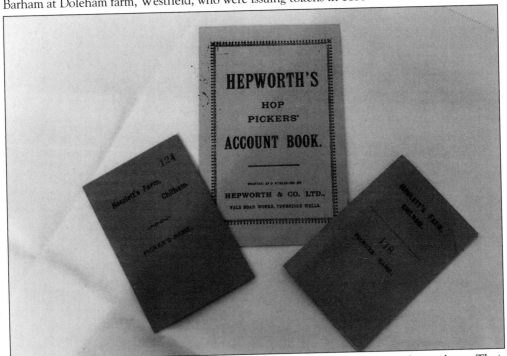

Some farms preferred to issue Hoppers with their own tally book, rather than tokens. Their daily tally was also entered in the farm account book. Some farmers were more generous than others when it came to measuring the bushel baskets and recording the tallies; others expected pickers to 'pick the hops well, to their employer's satisfaction', which allowed for no leeway in interpreting the farmer's requirements.

REGULATIONS AND RULES

To be observed by all persons engaged, either as Measurers, Pole-Pullers, or Pickers, by Alfred May, at his farm.

MEASURERS.—To keep order in the hop-grounds ; to prevent all quarrelling and disorderly conduct ; to cause the undermentioned regulations to be properly carried into effect ; to keep true accounts of all forfeits that may have been incurred ; to require the binmen to draw for their sets when advised by the measurers ; to attend properly and fairly to the pickers, and to take care only ten basketfuls be put in a poke ; in measuring, to fill his basket full, but as lightly as possible, and to measure as often as may be necessary for the convenience of the pickers, in regular order, without preference to any person, and to take no half-baskets except on Saturday.

POLE-PULLERS.—Wages to be three shillings per day, or in proportion thereto for the time he may be employed ; to be in the hop-gardens by six o'clock in the morning ; to pull poles to 8 bins of pickers and require them to pick their hops well and to pick up all hops dropped near their bins ; to use the hop-dog, and not to break any poles through careless-ness or negligence ; to assist the measurer ; to carry off the pokes and load the same on the wagon whenever required ; to assist the other pole-pullers at the last measuring of the day. For every breach of these regulations the pole-puller shall forfeit threepence. To take care of the bins, clothes, pokes and hop-dog committed to his charge, and to deliver up the same at the end of the picking, or on leaving his place ; on default thereof to pay the cost of replacing what may be missing or unfairly damaged. If discharged for bad conduct, or for not observing these regulations, to forfeit one day's wages.

HOP-PICKERS.—All pickers to pick the hops well, to their em-ployer's satisfaction, and to be subject to the regulations herein set forth ; and after the tally shall have been set, they are to remain until the picking is all finished ; to pick up all hops dropped near their bins, and to have their hops ready for the measurer, so that no delay may arise ; to be in the hop-gardens and to remain there at the appointed hours. For every breach of these Regulations to forfeit one basket of hops. Any pickers who shall leave before the picking is finished, or who shall be discharged for conduct not in accordance with the foregoing Regulations, or for other misconduct, shall be paid off at the rate of one shilling for every 12 baskets.

GENERAL REGULATIONS.—Signal to be given by blowing a horn or otherwise when the picking is to be commenced or left off. No hops to be picked during dinner time ; no lucifer matches to be used within the distance of five hills from a bin ; no smoking allowed near the buildings or premises ; no fire or light to be used after nine o'clock in the evening ; no spirituous liquors to be sold or bought in the hop gardens ; no abusive, improper or immoral language to be made use of ; and no quarreling or fighting to take place. For any breach of these general orders the person offending shall forfeit one shilling. All forfeits to be taken account of by the measurer at the time, and the amount to be deducted from the sums due to the offender when paid at the finish of the picking.

No picker allowed in the stackyards, or in the oasthouses, and not to touch any pokes. No picker to touch any wood except that allotted to him. For every breach of the above rules the offender to forfeit 6d. The Tally to be set at the beginning of the picking, and no picker allowed to draw more than 1d. per basket during the picking.

'Rules is Rules' and these applied to Hoppers, too. Mrs C. Reeve was a Hopper at Alfred May's farm where pickers were issued with their own set of rules on the back of their tally card. The undated card was issued at a time when 'lucifers' (easily-ignited phosphorus-headed matches which were both unreliable and dangerous) were in common use. Hoppers were ordered to begin or cease work by the blowing of a horn. It is clearly stated that anyone disobeying the rules would be fined for doing so.

113

	Mrs. Arky Well.	(117) Picker.								

DATE.	MEASURINGS.					TOTAL.	TALLY.	CASH PAID.		
	1	2	3	4	5			£	s.	d.
	4	5	2			11	7			
	4	3	5			13				
	5	1	2			8				
	1	3	6			10				
	6	3	4			13				
	4	6	8	3		16				
						7	3			
						£1		4		7

The Hopper's tally card was printed on the reverse of May's farm's rules. Each line shows the number of times the tallyman stopped by the bins to record their reckoning , and also the number of bushels marked down to the family at each visit. Each line is totalled, and an over all total is recorded beneath the tallying. At the bottom is the amount to be paid for their tally of bushels. The value of £1.4s.7d is £1.22½p in today's money. The pickers were paid about 1½d per bushel.

Oast designs vary from one county to another, according to the designers. In Kent, oasts may have round, square or even octagonal kilns. Modern cowls are made of fibreglass as it can cost around £300 to have one made in wood in the traditional way. With the tiling removed, it is easy to see the basic structural design of the round oast, as seen from the drying floor.

Once, and sometimes twice a week enterprising shopkeepers such as Mr Aldridge in 1920, and assistants Arthur and Charlie, trundled their wares down to the hop gardens, sometimes from as far as the East End of London. They set up a make-shift counter and sold supplies to the Hoppers. These included groceries, bread and buns, vegetables and ice cream. Travelling Tinkers visited the farms, too, cycling along the lanes with their bikes strung with ribbons, laces, elastic and buttons, as well as with pots, pans and patches. A holed enamel bucket or tin kettle could be mended by the simple application of two tin discs with a washer between, screwed tightly through the hole by a small nut and bolt at sixpence ($2\frac{1}{2}$ d) for each hole repaired.

The last call of the day was 'pull no more bines', when Hoppers would clear up any hops dropped around their bins, leaving their pitch tidy and ready for the next day. At the end of the Season when the last bine was about to be pulled, Hoppers on many farms held a ceremony. This varied from the tallymen and measurers being carried back to the farm, shoulder high, to the appointing and crowning of a Hop Queen, crowned with a circlet of hops and dressed in a cloak before being pulled to a Hop Ball or party held on the last night. In George Thirkell's picture, two bine hooks can be seen, about to be used for ceremoniously cutting down the last bine.

Hop-washing machinery was regularly used to spray the hops with diluted liquid sulphur to kill off any fungus or blight settling on the bines. Once a disease took hold it could rapidly spread throughout the Hop Garden, ruining the whole crop and infecting nearby farms.

THE HOP AND MALT
EXCHANGE.

THE new building in Southwark-street, Borough designed for a Hop and Malt Exchange, has just been opened for the business of the trade. It has been constructed by a limited liability company, with an original capital of £120,000, the architect, Mr. R. H. Moore, of Walbrook, being one of the share-holders. It is situated near the London Bridge end of Southwark-street, opposite the Alliance Bank and the premises of the Hop Planters' Association. It has a frontage of 340 ft. in that street, and a 75-ft. frontage in Red Cross-street, the site comprising more than an acre of ground. In the front, Portland-stone pedestals, about 4 ft. 6 in. high, forming the base of cast-iron ornamental columns, extend the entire length, except at the ends and principal entrance. The entrance is flanked with pillars of Portland stone, in all about 27 ft. high. The build-ing consists of an Exchange-room, 80 ft. long by 50 ft. wide, and 75 ft. high to the cornice, from which springs an iron roof of 25 ft. radius, with a lantern-light sur-mounting it, and arrangements for ample ventilation. From the ridge of this lantern to the floor the height is 115 ft. The floor is laid with encaustic tiles. Around the Exchange are four stories of offices and show-rooms. The three upper floors are approached from ornamental cast-iron galleries running all round. The stone staircases at the opposite angles of the Exchange, and one at the prin-cipal entrance, lead up to the galleries, giving access to each office. The floors of the galleries, partly set with small squares of plate glass, are carried on brackets of appropriate design, in which, as well as the balcony railing, the hop leaf and seed have been introduced. The carvers are Frampton and Wil-liamson. A refreshment-room (first and second class) is provided; and a subscription-room, 40 ft. by 35 ft. and 24 ft. high, having a rich ceiling, with six glass star-lights. A fireproof gallery is carried along one end of this room, affording access to a set of offices fronting the street. The remaining portion of the building, yet unfinished, which will be built to its full height in about three months, will consist of warehouses and offices in the front, the height of four stories. There will be in all above one hundred offices, fifty show-rooms, sixty stands, be-sides basement offices for wine merchants and others, with ware-house-room for 50,000 bales of hops and other produce, and cellarage for about 3000 barrels of ale or other goods. The area of the warehouse-room for the storage of hop and other produce will exceed 220,000 superficial feet.

The cost of the entire building up to the present date is £40,000, and it is estimated that the part un-finished will cost about £10,000. It is anticipated that the rents will be not less than £3000 per annum. By the erection of this exchange, the hop growers, mer-chants, dealers, and buyers will have all the advantages of a com-plete and well-attended market close to the termini of all the rail-ways which pass through the hop-growing districts of Kent, Surrey, and Sussex, and will thus be en-abled to avoid the trouble, expense, and loss of time incurred in visiting hop merchants' counting-houses in various parts of the Borough.

THE NEW HOP AND MALT EXCHANGE.

Illus. London News. 26-10-186

The opulent Hop and Malt Exchange in Borough High Street, near London Bridge, newly built in 1867. Those hops not designated for direct delivery to specific buyers were sent here, mainly by rail, from the Hop Gardens and sold to the highest bidder. (*London Illustrated News*)

Eight

Champneys' Old Farm, Lamberhurst, Kent

Old Farm was established in the sixteenth century when the house was built, with it's graceful Elizabethan chimneys. In 1720 a barn was built close behind the house while two oast houses were added in 1830. The farm was bought in 1860 by Henry Owen Champneys, Professor of Botany at London University, as land over which he could go shooting, and remains much the same today as it was then. The attached hop gardens were leased out to hop farmers until 1927, when his son Henry took over and administered them himself.

Henry Champneys at Old Farm.

Henry Champneys, wife Joan and son Adam outside the main door of the farm with Willy and Sonny, their springer spaniels.

Adam in the vegetable garden in the 1950s. Behind him are one of the oast houses and an espalier fruit tree growing against the Elizabethan chimney breast. The tree was the same height as this when the Champneys first moved to Old Farm in 1860. Oast houses are a familiar sight in Kent. While many are now converted to modern dwellings, some are still used for their original purpose of storing, drying and pressing hops.

Hoppers at Old Farm were local people. Only a few came down from London. Local ladies, Mrs Baldock, Mrs Thrift and Mrs Davis stop to enjoy an afternoon tea break. Two empty pokes lie on the ground beside them ready to be filled in the afternoon picking session.

Albert Midmore of Old Farm adjusts Nobby's bridle after winning 2nd Prize in the Lamberhurst Horse Show Open Class. Nobby was normally used for 'muck-spreading' between the hop rows but his moment of glory came in Summer of 1946 . Albert has dressed him smartly with ribbons and cockade to present him at his best for the show.

Henry Champneys filling a bushel basket as he checks the pickings of his Hoppers. Tom Clout holds a poke ready to be filled. Albert and Tom still work at Old Farm.

Adam Champneys on the cooling room floor with the scuppet used to load dried hops into the hop press. This was known as 'scuppeting'. On the wooden boards behind him are some of the date stencillings used for the hop pockets. Each pocket had to be date- stamped according to the rules of the Hop and Malt Marketing Board. This was to prevent farmers from passing off the previous years' crop as freshly harvested.

Standing on the kiln floor of an oast with the inside the drying floor above. The holes in the upper floor, some of which is missing, allowed moisture to escape from the drying hops. These were regularly turned, using a Hop Spud (form). Driers got to know the vagaries of their kilns, and heaped or thinned the hops according to where they knew the heat rose most or least.

The Champneys' hop press. The top edge of a fresh pocket was fixed inside the round hole beneath the press. This was filled to capacity with dried hops from the cooling room, behind, then the press was wound down into the pocket, ramming the hops down tightly. The press was then raised to allow more hops to be shovelled in, using a scuppet, before being rammed tight again. This continued until the pocket had just sufficient room left at the top to tie two 'ears' for lifting. The two pieces of wood across the hole have been put in place temporarily, to prevent anyone falling down the hole. They would not be there when the press was in use.

John Heffernan working the geared press. Adam Champneys stands behind.

Hop pockets were supported from below by a strong leather sling to counteract the pressure being given by the press. When the pocket was full, it was sewn across the top by hand using special coping twine. This method has not been improved upon and is still in use.

Adam Champneys and John Heffernan viewing one of the drying floors from an overhead wooden landing joining the two oast houses. The lath and plaster construction can be seen clearly.

It was common for pre World War One and earlier hop-pickers to take a small cask or 'firkin' of cider or ale with them to the fields for refreshment. John stands in front of Old Farm's Elizabethan fireplace with his cider firkin ready for a day's work. Behind him, Harry the distinguished farmhouse cat sitting in the perambulator, shares Queen Anne Boleyn's unusual attribute of having six digits.

Adam climbing to the doors leading to two drying floors above the oil-fired kilns. The dryer, on duty 24 hours to keep the temperature gauges under constant observation throughout the process, usually slept near his furnaces. Early kilns were wood fuelled, later, by charcoal. Modern furnaces are oil-fired. Until the 1980s, sticks of sulphur were added to the fires: the fumes gave hops the yellowish tint demanded by brewers. There was a strong belief that children's blood needed thinning in summer. 'Brimstone and treacle' was an unpopular medicine for this; a tablespoonful of black treacle dipped into flowers of sulphur and swallowed straight off left an unforgettably dry taste on the tongue.

John checking one of the furnaces. Above his head is the furnace's temperature gauge and to his right is the heat control handle.

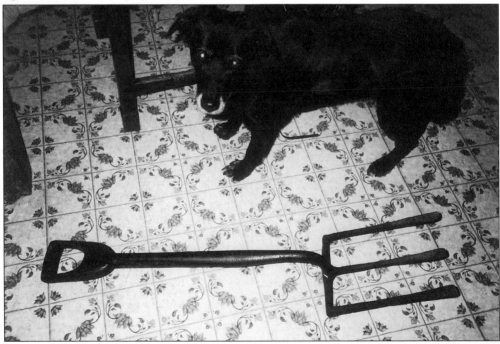

Old Polly guards a Hop Spud or fork, strongly made of iron with an extra long iron sheath covering the wooden shaft. Blunting the tines helped avoid damaging the hops when turning them on the drying floor.Once dried, hops were raked onto the cooling floor and regularly turned, using the special fork. At the same time, hops were checked for signs of mould.

John and Adam hold up a fresh hop pocket in the Champneys' Elizabethan kitchen. Made of fine sacking, pockets are twill-woven for strength to counteract the pressure produced by the hop press. Three sides are firmly oversewn using thick coping twine.

Outside the Champneys' twin oasts and drying shed are the oil tanks used to fuel the two kilns, one in the base of each tower. Two loading doors are in the upper part of the shed, leading directly to the cooling floor which extends the length of the building. Oasts are divided into four or five areas, according to design. The poke store was at ground level, below the cooling room. From stowage, hops were taken up to the open slatted green stages and tipped onto porous matting, usually hessian, ready to be spread out on the drying floor above the kiln.

Acknowledgements

My thanks go to the following contributors
who supplied pictures from their private collections:

Mr M.E. Amos, Mr Michael Ash, Mrs Phyllis Ash, Mr Kim Beaton, Mr Duncan Bennock,
Mrs Patricia Boyce, Emily Braidwood, Sidney Cave, Jan and Adam Champneys,
Richard W. Cliffe, Mrs L.M. Chittenden, Mrs Evelyn Diddell, Miss Dunsden,
Harry and Harriet Edwards, Mr C. Eldridge, Mrs Kath Embleton, Mr Arthur T. Ellis,
Mrs Alice Evans, Mrs D. Fairman, Alice Fullerton, Mrs Q. Garrett Mr Frank Green,
Mrs K. Harrison, Mr Ken Higgs, Mr Fred Holtum, Mrs Hull, Mr A.M. Hull, Mr F.J. Jex,
Mr and Mrs Kennard, Mrs Ann Lee, Mr Albert G. Lloyd, Mrs A. Lovell, Mrs G.E. Mason,
Mrs Pauline Mayern, Mr Newton, Mrs B. Perkins, Mr Cyril Perrier, Mr F. Redknap,
Mr Ron Riley, Miss C. Reeve, Mr and Mrs Rose, Mr H.W. Sheppard, Mr Bill Shrieve,
Mrs D. Simmons, Mrs Pat Skinner, Mrs E.A. Slater, Mrs Viola Summers, Mr George Thirkell,
Mr Alan Turpin, Mr Bill White, Alice and Fred Wood

My sincere thanks for their assistance and co-operation go to
Octavia Haywood-Kenny and staff, Kent Museum for Rural Life, Cobtree, Kent,
for permission to use the photographs on pp. 24, 25, 41 (top), 99, 104 (top and bottom),
105 (top and bottom), 106 (top and bottom), 107 (top and bottom), 108 (top and bottom),
110 (top), 114, 116, 117
Janice Brooker and Len Riley of Southwark Local History Studies Library,
211 Borough High St, London SE1 1JA, for permission to use the photographs
on pp. 2, 10, 11, 14, 15 (top and bottom), 16 (top and bottom), 17, 18 (top and bottom),
19 (top and bottom), 20, 21, 23 (bottom), 26, 41 (bottom), 42, 115, 118
J.D. Butterworth, The National Farmers Union, North Kent
Joy Toghill, The Danson Youth and Community Centre, Bexleyheath, Kent
Richard Stutely, Maidstone Borough Council, Kent
Age Exchange, Reminiscence Centre, Blackheath, South London
Mrs Todd, M.D. Whitbreads Hop Farm, Paddock Wood, Kent
London Illustrated News
Fox Studios, London

Finally, my thanks and apologies go to anyone whose material or help has contributed to this
book's production but whom I have inadvertently failed to acknowledge by name.

*Sylvia Harper ('The Capuchin Friars of Erith' in Bygone Kent) says the Friars tended the
Catholics working in Paddock Wood, Marden, Staplehurst, Yalding, Hunton and
Wateringbury Hopgardens.